604

SUSSEX
A portrait in colour

ANDY WILLIAMS
with text by Brigid Chapman

COUNTRYSIDE BOOKS

For Alice

First published 1989
© Andy Williams 1989
Revised and reprinted 1993, 1999

COUNTRYSIDE BOOKS
3 CATHERINE ROAD
NEWBURY, BERKSHIRE

ISBN 1 85306 027 5

Produced through MRM Associates Ltd., Reading
Typeset by Acorn Bookwork, Salisbury
Printed in Singapore

Contents

Beachy Head Lighthouse – Front Cover

Many a sailor's life has been saved by the light that shines for 25 miles out to sea from the lighthouse at the foot of Beachy Head. As long ago as 1670 there was a light on this 300ft high cliff which ends the 80 mile long line of the South Downs from the Hampshire border. Then in 1828 James Walker built a 47ft high circular stone tower on the clifftop but the light in it was often obscured by fog or low cloud while the air below was quite clear. However, it remained in use until 1899 when it was decided that a new lighthouse was needed, particularly as the weight of the existing one was likely to cause the cliff to collapse at any moment. The present tower is 142ft high and the white group flashing light 103ft above the level of mean high water. In fog an electrically powered signal sounds every 30 seconds.

Singleton – Back Cover

This miniature town on the fringe of the forest that covers the southern slope of the Downs is enclosed by hills crowned with clumps of trees. Under one of them, the Trundle, so it is said, there is treasure in the form of a golden calf. But one must not dig for it or it will disappear. ... The church with its large Saxon west tower stands among houses and cottages with walled gardens and ponds the size of small lakes. In it is a tablet to the memory of Thomas Johnson who died in 1744. He was huntsman of the Charlton Hunt, the most premier pack in the country in the reign of William III, and took part in a famous ten hour chase in January 1738 when dukes, lords, knights and gentlemen of the shire followed the 23 Charlton hounds from Eastdean Wood to the banks of the Arun at South Stoke in pursuit of a vixen.

The River Ouse at Lewes

Introduction

God gave all men all earth to love
But since man's heart is small,
Ordains for each one spot shall prove
Beloved over all.

Each to his choice, and I rejoice
The lot has fallen to me
In a fair ground – in a fair ground –
Yea, Sussex by the sea!

There is not a band in Sussex – brass, silver, town or Scottish pipe – that does not have *Sussex By The Sea* in its repertoire. This tune by Ward Higgs is played to welcome civic dignitaries to civic ceremonies; it is played in carnival processions, at fetes, flower shows and fairs. For the people of Sussex are proud of their county which some still like to call a kingdom. It was one from AD 491 when a Saxon chieftain called Aella exterminated the last Britons at Anderida and declared himself king of the South Saxons. Before that time it was part of the Roman Empire. The legions marched along the crest of the Downs between the fortified port of Anderida and the city of Noviomagus or Regnum, now Chichester. They also built a good straight Roman road, Stane Street, to Londinium.

Until the coaching era, the roads the Romans built were the only means of access to the county from the north for thick forest extended along the northern border from Wessex to Kent. So most visitors came by sea. The most remembered is still William, Duke of Normandy, who defeated Harold of England at the Battle of Hastings in 1066.

William landed at Pevensey and immediately strengthened the castle the Romans had built in the settlement they called Anderida, before moving along the coast to build his own stronghold on the cliffs at Hastings. After his victory he ordered an abbey to be built on the site of the conflict – at Battle.

He also ordered a survey to be made of the country he had conquered. In 1086 it was completed and was arranged by counties and by the landowners within those counties. In the Domesday Book 14 landholders are listed for Sussex among them the king, the Archbishop of Canterbury, various abbots and bishops, counts and earls. The survey was nothing if not thorough. They even counted the eels in the manor of South Malling on the outskirts of Lewes. There were 2,000 – as well as 219 villagers with 35 smallholders having 73 ploughs and 43 crofts and 300 pigs for pasturage.

Sussex remained in its Domesday Book mode for centuries. But gradually the forests of the Weald were cut down and more land cleared for sheep, cattle and corn. As trade improved the towns grew, the ports expanded and a road system developed.

Industry came to the county in the 16th century and brought wealth to some people. Charcoal was the fuel for the furnaces of the iron founders who forged the cannon which scattered the Armada. Everywhere the woods were cut down and furnaces blazed away producing the best iron in the world and some good glass and gunpowder. This industry, which lasted some 200 years (the last furnace closed down at Ashburnham in 1809) totally changed the topography. No longer were communications only easy by sea or along the coastal strip, for the turnpike roads were beginning to snake southward through the devastated Weald and the people of the capital began coaching to the coast.

The Cinque Ports, a confederacy of five maritime towns set up by William the Conqueror to provide ships when called upon for the defence of the realm, had declined in power since Tudor times. Their fishermen went back to fishing instead of fighting the French although the officers of the confederacy are still required to perform certain ceremonial duties. Today the Lord Warden of the Cinque Ports is the Queen Mother.

The Sussex shore has lost its shipping, except at Newhaven and Shoreham, but has replaced it with something vastly more profitable – visitors. In 1750 Dr Richard Russell of Lewes wrote a dissertation on the benefits to health of bathing in sea water and the trek to the coast began. Dr Johnson was at Brighton in 1765 and in 1783 the 21 year old Prince of Wales, later George IV drove down to visit his uncle, the Duke of Cumberland who had taken a house there for the summer.

The prince fell in love at first sight with Sussex by the sea and was soon converting the farmhouse he had first rented and later bought into a villa and then to the Oriental pleasure dome that is the Royal Pavilion. Where the prince went, society followed. It was six hours by coach from London to the coast and little fishing villages changed into resorts almost overnight. Eastbourne was patronised by some more of George III's children, and royalty descended on Worthing and Bognor, which narrowly avoided having its name changed to Hothampton.

First came the princes, then the people, brought by the new railway which linked London first with Brighton and then with other towns along the coast. Sussex did everything it could to welcome them and cater for their requirements as it has done for its visitors throughout history. Soon the day trippers were followed by the developers, many of them local builders, who cashed in quickly on the need for holiday and retirement homes. Peacehaven, nearly called Anzac on Sea, sprang up between Brighton and Newhaven; bungalows and villas were built westward from Worthing to Rustington; and caravan sites blossomed round Bracklesham Bay. Bognor got Butlins.

Away from the coast Sussex hardly changed at all. The more scenically enchanting villages, and there were many of them, probably boasted a tea shop and occasionally a 'Coaches Welcome' sign would go up outside the village inn. Fast trains to London attracted commuters to the new residential centres of Haywards Heath and Crowborough but the newcomers were quickly absorbed into the life of the locality. Many a City banker or merchant would exercise his power over matters of money on weekdays and be out for a duck to the blacksmith's bowling on the village green at the weekend.

Then in 1939 blacksmith and banker went off to war. The men and women of Sussex whose ancestors had watched for Napoleon from the clifftops and Martello towers in the early 1800s now faced invasion by a different enemy.

It did not come but the bombers did and after them the flying bombs. The first high explosive bombs of the war fell on Ticehurst on May 22, 1940. The first flying bomb fell near Haywards Heath on June 13, 1944.

Sussex took some hard knocks in the war. It lost many of its sons and daughters, a few of its interesting old buildings, a whole lot of its houses. But its soul – and its scenery – have survived. See for yourselves.

Brigid Chapman

Bosham Harbour

The wooded waterside village of Bosham was once one of the chief towns of Sussex. Vespasian, commander of the Second Legion had a villa here during the Roman Occupation and in the seventh century an Irish monk called Dicul built the first church in Sussex on its shore and set out to convert the South Saxons to Christianity. He had little success, for the Saxons proved difficult to convert. 'Will be led, won't be druv' has always been the county motto.

And it was from Bosham in 1064 that Earl Godwin's son Harold embarked to visit William, Duke of Normandy – a visit William was to return with interest in 1066. The Bayeux Tapestry, which records in needlework the Norman Conquest and the events that led up to it, shows Harold visiting Bosham church, drinking in the village alehouse and boarding his galley accompanied by assorted soldiery.

Another king whose name is linked in legend with Bosham is Canute. Certainly he was here with his father, Svein the Dane, on a raid in 1049 but it is doubtful that he had a manor here, that his daughter is buried in the church and that his famous confrontation with the tide took place in the estuary.

It was during one of these raids by the Danes that the bells from the church were carried off as plunder. But they did not get far. The galley carrying them foundered under their weight and sank to the bottom of the sea. Today, it is said, whenever a peal is rung on the present bells, it is answered by a peal from the deep . . .

At high water Bosham is beautiful. Boats bob at anchor or sail about the bay – it is a scene that has inspired many a contributor to the Royal Academy summer exhibitions. The only people not to appreciate it are the unfortunates who, like Canute, make a miscalculation about the tide and return to find the cars they had parked on dry land are over their wheels in water.

The sea complains upon a thousand shores.
Alexander Smith

Chichester Market Cross

Chichester's Gothic market cross was a gift to the city from Bishop Edward Story (1478–1503) to provide shelter for the poor who brought their produce to sell beneath it. It is built, like much of the cathedral, of Caen stone and is a mass of arches, buttresses, pinnacles and other adornments. Until the Civil War, when they were destroyed by the Parliamentarians, there were a number of statues in niches beneath the present belfry which dates from 1724. The four clock dials were installed in 1746.

Like most cathedral cities Chichester has plenty of precincts, cloisters, gardens and closes. A few steps away from its busy four main streets, now pedestrianised, are quiet rows of Georgian fronted houses. Even the car parks are havens of tranquillity, surrounded as they are by trees, shrubs and borders of flowers.

It has changed successfully with the times but has not totally obliterated its past. The dice used in a Roman gaming room are now on show in the Dolphin and Anchor which was once two coaching inns – the Whig Dolphin and Tory Anchor; the licensee of the Royal Arms still brews a milk punch from a hundred year old recipe; and the room in Lord Lumley's Scarborough House where Elizabeth I held audiences has been carefully preserved in all its baroque splendour.

The 277ft high spire of the cathedral towers above the city and the flat plain on which it is built. Its grace and its simplicity are echoed in the verses of Chichester's greatest poet, William Collins.

With eyes up-raised, as one inspired,
Pale Melancholy sat retired;
And, from her wild sequestered seat,
In notes by distance made more sweet,
Poured through the mellow horn her pensive soul.
William Collins

Selsey

The men of Selsey have been fishing ever since St Wilfrid was cast up on the Sussex shore, converted the pagan inhabitants to Christianity and taught them how to net fish — a skill he had acquired in his native Northumbria. The church St Wilfrid built was drowned by the encroaching sea about 800 years ago and further flooding in the 16th century submerged a large deer park. But the memory of it remains alive in local tradition and the people of Selsey still speak of the area as the park. Now they fish it rather than poach it which they did to such an extent in the reign of Henry VIII that they were excommunicated by bell, book and candle from every church in the diocese. The present church of St Peter once stood much nearer the sea. It was moved stone by stone, each one numbered, to its present site in the 19th century. Only the chancel of the 13th century church which replaced St Wilfrid's cathedral was left to weather away in the fields.

In the summer Selsey is alive and bustling with holidaymakers. It is particularly favoured by caravanners and campers and families with young children in search of sea, sun and sand. In the winter only the locals remain and the fishermen carry on fishing. Chichester lobsters, most of which come from Selsey, are among the traditional good things of Sussex, along with Amberley trout and Arundel mullet. On fine days the shallow waters round Selsey Bill, the southernmost tip of the county, look so safe and tranquil. But even on the sunniest summer day dense banks of fog can suddenly appear to blot out all sight of land for anyone afloat and confuse all sounds. A number of lives have been saved in recent years by the Selsey lifeboat, the Tyne class City of London.

The sea moans over dead men's bones.
T.B. Aldrick

Glorious Goodwood

Glorious Goodwood, that week in July when the world of racing comes to Sussex, the sun always shines and everyone's a winner, had a decidedly shaky start. It was launched in 1802 by the 3rd Duke of Richmond and Gordon, he who built the Martello towers along the coast when Napoleon threatened to invade. He also spent vast sums on extending Goodwood House to its present magnificence and died with debts of £150,000. Before the 1803 meeting at Goodwood the stewards were forced to announce that they could not provide £50 for the handicap sweepstake because many of the promised subscriptions to the racing fund had not been paid.

Royal interest in racing revived Goodwood's fortunes. Edward VII and Queen Alexandra brought the Prince of Wales (later George V) and his wife down in 1903 to stay at Goodwood House. 'Numerous dainties for the table' were sent down from Windsor and some items of furniture from Buckingham Palace. They were here again in 1904 and 1905 and the king was a winning owner of the Sussex Stakes with *Minoru*, ridden by Herbert Jones.

It was not only horses which lined up at the start between 1948 and 1966. A motor racing circuit was established by the 5th Duke of Richmond and Gordon, a well known racing driver of the 1930s, on the wartime airfield of Westhampnett. The rich and famous would come by air to watch the Formula One monsters hurtle through the chicane. The setting of the circuit was scenically superb but, as speeds got faster and faster the potential danger for spectators increased so much the motor racing had to stop. Today the track is used for testing and trials plus the occasional vintage car event. The Champagne shaking champions are there no longer, alas.

The horse thinks one thing, and he that rides him another.
Proverb

Bognor Regis

Bognor is friendly, compact, cheerful. It has a sandy beach and goes in for guest houses rather than huge hotels. To further its family holiday image, it once brought on the clowns! It was in April 1985 that the first Clowns Convention came to this seaside resort and the resulting festival of fun was voted a huge success. Arun District Council was only too happy to repeat the experiment and the Convention became an annual event, attracting clowns from all parts of the world to a Big Top which seated 1,500 spectators.

Sir Richard Hotham, the London hatter who decided in 1787 to build Bognor as a rival to Brighton, probably would not have liked it at all. He wanted to attract the rich, the famous and better still, the royals, to his new town which he threatened to call Hothampton. He did entice Princess Charlotte down for a holiday but her father, then Prince Regent, remained firmly in Brighton.

Bognor became Bognor Regis when King George V was brought to Craigweil by ambulance on February 9th, 1928 to convalesce after a serious illness. For four months Craigweil was a royal residence and Queen Mary would often be seen shopping for antiques in the neighbourhood or visiting Bognor bookshops to buy thrillers for the king. Other members of the royal family came to stay, among them three year old Princess Elizabeth, King George's favourite grandchild, and the dashing young Prince of Wales who flew to Bognor by private plane. How Sir Richard Hotham would have loved it.

> If all good people were clever
> And all clever people were good
> The world would be nicer than ever
> We thought that it possibly could.
> *Elizabeth Wordsworth*

Arundel Castle

The crenellated towers of Arundel Castle with their arrow slit windows keep up the medieval image of this feudal town. They look as if they have been there forever but they were built only about 100 years ago by the 15th Duke of Norfolk.

There has been a castle here since around 1070 when the town was a thriving port. An early owner was the evil Robert de Belleme, described by the chroniclers of the 12th century as a 'monster of iniquity and in cruelty pre-eminent among the savages of the age'. He was attainted and stripped of all his possessions. His castle was claimed by the crown and King Henry I willed it to his queen, Adeliza, who later married William d'Aubigny (or de Albini) third Earl of Arundel. King Stephen half heartedly besieged the castle when Adeliza took in her stepdaughter, Matilda, a rival claimant for the throne but the real damage to it was done in 1643 by the Parliamentarians under Sir William Waller. They reduced a lot of it to rubble by cannonfire and occupied the remains until 1649. The castle passed from the d'Aubignys to the Fitzalans and in the 16th century to Thomas Howard, fourth Duke of Norfolk, Earl Marshal and senior peer of England. His heirs and successors have, except for the Civil War period, lived there ever since.

The castle is surrounded, with the exception of the river side where the town creeps right up to its walls, by a park of 1,100 acres. Here, every time a Test team visits this country, it plays the first match of the tour against the Duke's – or the Duchess's – XI, which usually includes a number of Sussex county players. And here also is Swanbourne Lake, its clear waters sparkling between the tree-covered sides of the combe. It is a scene that has been the subject of paintings by Constable, Turner, Vicat Coles and many other artists.

If you have built castles in the air, your work need not be lost; that is where they should be. Now put the foundations under them.

Thoreau

Cottages at Fittleworth

Fittleworth is a village with close connections with the art and music of Victorian and Edwardian England. The chocolate box prettiness it had in those days appealed to the painters of the period. The public for which they painted liked its pictures pretty and with a touch of sentimentality about them. First to set up his easel here was Vicat Coles. He rented a large house in the village called Brinkwells and held sketching classes for his friends. His social circle was a wide one and soon many artists were coming down by stage coach or post chaise for weekends in the country with him.

Even more arrived in the 1880s when Fittleworth station was opened and 18 trains a day on the Horsham to Pulborough line stopped at it. They were made welcome at the Swan, an old coaching inn run by Miss Jane Hawkins. She had a fondness for artists and not only persuaded them to patronise her house but also to paint in it. On the oak panels in the Picture Room of the inn are to this day paintings by John Varley, S G Burgess, Harold Cheesman, George Constable, Edward Knight, Edward Handley Reed, Augustus Weedon and other 19th and early 20th century artists. Also still on display is the inn sign painted by Robert Caton Woodville, noted for his scenes of conflict in the Boer War. Assisted by his son he produced a sign to hang from the centre of a wooden arch which spanned the village street. It showed a naked Leda, with a face remarkably like Queen Victoria's, sitting on the back of a swan. But propriety prevailed and the design was altered to show a well-draped faerie queen.

Modern Fittleworth still has its charming cottages, its tile hung houses, its beautiful gardens. The station has long since closed and the artists have gone, but a melody lingers. A group of chamber music by Edward Elgar bears the inscription 'Brinkwells in 1918' for the composer rented the house for a holiday and wrote some string quartets there which later he used as the theme for his 'cello concerto.

There is room in the smallest cottage for a happy loving pair.
Schiller

Worthing

Worthing should be seen from the sea. The modern town, which has a multi-storey car park on its promenade, looks at its best against the backdrop of the rolling Downs which protect it from the cold north winds in winter. It was the arrival of royalty that launched Worthing as a seaside resort, as it did Brighton. But whereas Brighton got the Prince of Wales, later to become George IV, and the glittering social scene that he created, Worthing got his ailing sister Amelia who liked a quiet life; her aged mother Queen Charlotte; her unfortunate sister-in-law Queen Caroline; and later Queen Adelaide.

The town's major expansion came with the railway. Soon its genial climate, level ground, good sands – when the tide is out – and the hinterland of the Downs attracted holidaying families from all parts of the country. They liked what they saw and many decided to settle. For the builders it was boom time and bungalows and villas, even Moorish mansions, sprang up from Lancing to the far reaches of Ferring. The retired moved into them in droves and postwar prosperity increased their numbers so much that the label Costa Geriatrica was unkindly applied to the area and the borough council began to do something about the age imbalance.

Today the borough of Worthing has a resident population of some 100,000 and does a brisk holiday trade as well. It has played host to the World Bowls in the park opposite Beach House where playwright Edward Knoblock used to live. But the house in which Oscar Wilde spent a three week holiday in September 1894 and wrote *The Importance of Being Earnest* has disappeared, as has the rest of the town's early architecture. There are shopping malls and pedestrian precincts where once there was a theatre, an assembly hall and two rival hotels, one run by a Mr Hogsflesh, the other by Mrs Bacon. But a Victorian lamp-post has been preserved and Grade II listed as of historic or architectural interest.

I grow old, I grow old
I shall wear the bottoms of my trousers rolled
Shall I part my hair behind? Do I care to eat a peach?
I shall wear white flannel trousers and walk upon the beach.
                                                                T.S. Eliot

The River Arun at Pulborough

At Pulborough two former links with London meet. A four arched stone bridge carries the Roman Stane Street across the river Arun, once part of the Wey and Arun canal on which cargoes were carried from the coast to the capital. Today there are more reminders of Pulborough's Roman past than of its relatively short career as a town with a waterborne trade. Remains of Roman villas have been unearthed and a temple and a mausoleum have been discovered along Stane Street.

It was in 1785 that the Arun Navigation Company first started to dredge the river above Arundel and for some 20 years from around 1830 coal, china clay and slate were carried by barge from Littlehampton to London. The canals, viaducts, tunnels and locks of the Wey and Arun Canal were used for the last time in 1871. Competition from the railways had killed the canal and for the next 100 years it was virtually forgotten. Its tunnels caved in, its viaducts collapsed, its locks crumbled away and whole sections were built over. In the 1970s a scheme to restore the waterway was launched and for years volunteers have been toiling away at weekends to get the locks working again and to dredge out channels long silted up. While this work goes on the Arun continues to flow peacefully through Pulborough with not a single bit of commercial traffic to disturb the many anglers who line its banks.

The Swan Inn by the bridge has had the river in its cellar many times for the low lying water meadows to the south are prone to flooding although the Water Board has done its best to ease the annual inundation.

He who knows not his way straight to the sea should choose the river for his guide.

Plautus

Bignor Roman Villa

In 1811 tenant farmer George Tupper was ploughing a field called the Berry on Lord Newburgh's estate at Bignor when he turned up a mosaic pavement. That was the start of the excavation of a large Roman villa that was probably the home of a Colonial Governor around AD 400. The first mosaic to be uncovered was in what is now known as the Ganymede Room. Its decorated area is in two circular sections, one 7ft 6ins in diameter and the other 16ft. In the smaller circle Ganymede, most beautiful of mortals, is pictured being carried off by an eagle to Olympus to become cup bearer to Zeus. The larger circle contains six smaller designs showing figures of dancing nymphs in the centre of which is an hexagonal stone cistern four ft in diameter and 1ft 8ins deep. At the bottom of it is a three inch diameter lead pipe which runs off in a southerly direction. The path of the pipes of this room's central heating system can still be traced.

The Bignor villa has been excavated a number of times since its discovery in the early 19th century. Its lovely mosaics are protected from the weather by friendly little thatched huts and the site is still part of the surrounding farmland. Latest thinking is that the villa floored with the mosaics was the administrative centre of a 2,000 acre estate but ample evidence has been uncovered of an earlier timber framed structure on the site dating from around AD 200.

When I was young and wanted to see the sights,
They told me 'Cast an eye over the Roman camp
If you care to.'

Christopher Isherwood

ROOM 7
GANYMEDE & EAGLE

DANCERS MOSAIC

ROOM 7 - PISCINA (ORNAMENTAL WATER BASIN)

Petworth Deer Park

Petworth House is not in the centre of its park but at the southern end of it, practically in the town itself. Next to the massive entrance gates with its lodges is the church. Opposite the gates is a row of shops. Drivers taking the A285 north have a high wall screening the park on their left, but travellers on the A272 to Midhurst have a wonderful view of its green hills and valleys and its herds of deer. Much of it now belongs to the National Trust but when it was all owned by the third Lord Egremont, who allowed the title to die out by default, artists of the eminence of W J Turner were often entertained there. Turner preferred fishing in the lake to painting in the park but old Lord Egremont was prepared to wait. 'I want a picture when you have time, but remember, none of your damn nonsense' he would say – and he would get his picture of the sunset slanting over the parkland and the deer hazy in the distance.

The pictures Turner painted are in Petworth House together with the carvings of Grinling Gibbons, commissioned by the Duke of Somerset who built the house between 1688 and 1696. There are also portraits by Van Dyke of the Percys of Petworth including one of the Wizard Earl who had an interest in alchemy and was imprisoned in the Tower for 16 years for his suspected part in the Gunpowder Plot. These paintings are an important historical record, even the later ones such as the Turners. For the park he painted, with its tree lined avenues, looks very different today after the devastation it suffered on the night of October 16, 1987 when hurricane force winds swept across the county.

Every animal loves itself.
Cicero

Midhurst

In the quiet country town of Midhurst the curfew is still tolled each evening at eight from the church in memory, it is said, of a traveller who lost his way through the surrounding woods one dark and stormy night. It was the sound of the evening bell that led him to safety and in gratitude for his deliverance he left the income from some land to endow the ringing of the curfew in perpetuity.

Other reminders of the distant past include the 16th century Market House, and two famous inns. The Angel got its name from a group of emigrants on their way to Southampton to sail on the Mayflower to the New World. Tradition has it that they gave the name, the Angel, to each of the inns that received them kindly. The Spreadeagle, a former Tudor hunting lodge and now a three star hotel, is, according to Hilaire Belloc, 'the oldest and most revered of all the prime inns of the world'. Midhurst has a rather dubious electoral past. It was not exactly a rotten borough but it did return its two MPs with votes drawn from stones rather than from people. The right to vote was vested in certain tenancies and, when one of the Montagues demolished some of them to make room for the wall he wished to build around Cowdray Park, he kept the voting rights by writing 'A Burgage' on the stones that crossed the site of the tenements. These stones duly voted at each Parliamentary election.

It is hard to separate Midhurst from Cowdray, the burnt out shell of which still stands in dignified dereliction down by the river. Once Queen Elizabeth I was lavishly entertained here, her household consuming three oxen and 140 geese for breakfast. Nowadays it is the polo rather than the provender that brings Prince Charles to Cowdray Park.

Towns are the dwelling places of mortals; the gods
inhabit rural retreats.

Rousseau

Horsham

The face of Horsham has changed a lot in recent years. In the past 25 to 30 years the labyrinth of old streets in the town centre have been redeveloped. The old centre of the Carfax is still there and, carefully preserved in a flower-surrounded compound, is the iron ring used in bull baiting – a sport in which the local inhabitants have not indulged since it was banned in 1814. Beside the old there is the new. The courts and walks of yesterday have been converted to places where shopping is a pleasure and even the rain can be avoided.

Here and there old weatherboarded cottages, their gardens full of flowers in summer, still remain and at the end of the Causeway there is still St Mary's Church with its tall, twisty shingled spire and buttresses built in the 12th century. Inside is a tablet commemorating perhaps England's greatest lyric poet, who was born a few miles away at Field Place, Broadbridge Heath. It says simply: Percy Bysshe Shelley 1792 – 1822. A stone effigy of a noseless knight in armour lies near the altar. He is Thomas, Lord Braose, who died in 1395 and probably lost his nose to the Puritans some 200 years later. They had a rooted dislike of effigies.

The gabled 16th century Causeway House is now a museum with saddlers and wheelwrights shops, a forge and a Sussex kitchen. In the grounds is an 18th century barn where old agricultural machinery and tools are on display. Horsham was at one time the farming capital of West Sussex. People came here to buy their waggons and horses, their ploughs and their produce, and the local blacksmiths did an excellent trade in horseshoes – and in crossbows during the Hundred Years War. It was also famous for its roofing stone – those flat grey slabs so well loved by lichen, which adorn many of the old houses and cottages in the county. It is used no longer because its great weight needs the support of strong Sussex oak. Modern rafters apparently cannot cope.

Man's yesterday may ne'er be like his morrow:
Nought may endure but Mutability.
P.B. Shelley

Billingshurst

In the days when every parish church was packed on Sundays there was often competition for the best seats. At Billingshurst they even went so far as to have a pew race. A feud between two families had grown up over who should have the chancel seats and this divided the village. Every Sunday there would be an unseemly scramble by the rival families and their supporters for the prime positions. But at least it did not end in a duel as a similar pew feud did at Littlehampton in 1796.

Billingshurst's heyday was in the far past. It was an important station between Londinium and Regnum and the legions travelling along Stane Street would pause here for rest and refreshment – and no doubt some entertainment too. Even the name has a Roman origin, so it is said, being called after Belinus, an engineer who had to cut the way through the woods for Stane Street to be built. He is also credited with Billingsgate, through which the road entered London.

In the 18th century, according to Cobbett in his *Rural Rides*, Billingshurst was 'a very pretty village' and he had 'a very nice breakfast in a very neat little parlour of a very decent public house'. In the last few years Sotheby's in Sussex have moved their salerooms from Pulborough to Summers Place on the outskirts of the village and now, on sale and view days, the population is swollen by collectors and dealers from all over the world.

How often have I paused on every charm
The sheltered cot, the cultivated farm,
The never failing brook, the busy mill
The decent church that topt the neighbouring hill.
Oliver Goldsmith

Ye Olde Six Bells, Billingshurst

The Romans brought the public house to Sussex so it is only right that Billingshurst should have such a fine example of one in Ye Olde Six Bells. When the legions were using this village as a stopping place between their settlements to the north, south and east and west there was probably a house with a garland of vine leaves on a post outside it to indicate that there was wine within. Perhaps it was locally grown or imported from Gaul. This method of telling travellers where they could slake their thirst was continued by the Anglo Saxons with their ale stakes – the bunches of foliage they had to hang out whenever they had brewed ale for sale – and is continued to this day by inn signs.

Ye Olde Six Bells was originally a farmhouse, dating perhaps from the 15th century. It was later used as a lodging house for tramps and travellers who were presumably also served with ale. Only at the turn of the century did it become a fully licensed public house. Under its Horsham stone roof it has one of the largest stone flagged floors in the county – and also a puzzle from the past. In the main bar is a gravestone used as a fireback. It bears the inscription: 'Here lies Anne Forster, daughter and heir to Thomas Gaynsford, Esquire, deceased 18th January 1591, leaving behind her two sons and five daughters'. It is one of a number of Anne Forster tombstones used as firebacks. They all have the Ss and Fs upside down and reversed and the spelling and punctuation is archaic – not at all as it is transcribed here. Anne Forster was related to the Culpepers of Wakehurst Place and it is thought that the firebacks were placed in houses that she inherited from her father. Another piece of the past found at the pub was one of the original windows. When an extension was being built, workmen discovered the frame under some tiles they had stripped from a wall. It still had the nails that were used to hold fabric in place over the aperture before glass was in general use.

There is nothing which has yet been contrived by man, by which so much happiness is produced as by a good tavern or inn.

Samuel Johnson

Cowfold Church

Old timber framed houses and a cluster of cottages surround the parish church at Cowfold which attracts a steady stream of visitors, whatever the weather, whatever the season. They come to see one of the most beautiful sepulchral brasses in Sussex – that of Thomas Nelond, 25th prior of the Cluniac Priory of St Pancras at Lewes. No one knows how or why the brass, and perhaps his body, is in this medieval church a good 15 miles or so away from Lewes. Maybe it was brought here in the troubled times that followed Henry VIII's dissolution of the monasteries. The Lewes priory was broken up in 1538 and it could be that a dispossessed brother returned to his home village with this precious relic of monastic life. The brass would have been no easy object to transport. It is more than 10ft long and shows the life size figure of the old prior in his monk's habit with his arms clasped together in prayer. Surrounding him is an elaborate canopy on which are depicted the Virgin and Child, St Pancras and St Thomas a Becket. The brass is kept well covered with a thick carpet which is padlocked securely but there is a rubbing of it in the church for all to see.

A mile or so to the south rises the tall spire of the only active Carthusian monastery in this country – St Hugh's Charterhouse. It was built in 1877 on a grand scale for the white robed monks of the order founded by St Bruno, and for a time accommodated a number of French brothers who were fleeing from France to escape persecution. It has 34 rooms in its cloisters for the monks and 32 rooms for the lay brothers. Now some 20 to 30 monks spend their days in contemplation in their cells or hermitages, each of which has its own garden and workshop. They meet together only for services and for lunch on Sundays.

I have completed a monument more lasting than brass
Horace.

Leonardslee Gardens

The Victorians were not given to doing things by halves. When Sir Edmund Loder decided to take an interest in gardening he did not limit himself to an acre or two and a couple of greenhouses. In 1889 he bought Leonardslee at Lower Beeding, a garden originally begun in 1801, and set about planting this already well-wooded valley with the kinds of trees and shrubs which would give the best possible colour effects. It was all his own work: he did not employ a professional garden designer, and he developed his own hybrid rhododendrons – plants which, with camellias, were his particular favourites. Sir Edmund also introduced the wallabies which have been used as environmentally-friendly mowing machines in parts of the valley for over a hundred years.

Today Leonardslee is one of the largest and most spectacular woodland gardens in the country and has one of the finest collections of mature rhododendrons, trees and shrubs. From the end of April until early June the rhododendrons and azaleas are at their most magnificent. The gardens, now covering more than 200 acres, are open every day from the beginning of April until the end of October – when the autumn leaves are dazzling. The present owner of Leonardslee is Sir Edmund's great grandson Robin, who has carried on the tradition of planting the finest that is available.

At the bottom of the valley is a series of lakes created by the early iron founders in their excavations for ore, and they are breathtakingly beautiful in early summer when all the colours of the flowering shrubs are reflected in the water. There is a fine bonsai exhibition in the courtyard, while the Rock Garden (at its best in early May) has a superb collection of evergreen azaleas and two large Chinese Lantern trees.

A garden is a lovesome thing, God wot,
Fringed pool, ferned grot,
The veriest school of peace...
T.E. Brown

Brighton Beach

Since the first train steamed into Brighton's new station on September 21 1841 the town has been the first choice for Londoners wanting a day by the seaside. Of course, they used to come by stage coach before that but not in such numbers. Until Dr Richard Russell of Lewes published his treatise on the benefit to health of sea bathing, the men and women of this island race never thought of taking a dip for pleasure. The Channel was there to be fished or to be crossed to fight the French, not to swim in. Brighton made sea bathing its business in the 18th century and there was often a queue for the bathing machines lined up between the Old Ship Hotel and the bottom of West Street. They were presided over by the dippers, men and women who would spend their days up to their waists in water making sure that the belles and beaux of high society did not sink. Bathing attendant by royal appointment was Smoaker Miles who on one occasion stopped the Prince from having a swim as he considered the sea too rough. 'I'm not going to let the king hang me for letting the Prince of Wales drown himself' he said. Queen of the women dippers was Martha Gunn who lived to be 89 and is buried not far away in St Nicholas churchyard.

The days of a 60 minute run from Victoria in the Brighton Belle are over. Now it is a bumper to bumper crawl to the coast down the A23 on fine weekends – unless, of course, one comes by air and lands at nearby Shoreham or sails in to Brighton Marina. Brighton acts like a magnet to all who visit her.

Oh I do like to be beside the seaside
I do like to be beside the sea,
I do like to walk along the prom prom prom
And hear the brass band play tiddly om pom pom . . .
Popular Song

The Royal Pavilion, Brighton

The Royal Pavilion, that onion domed and minareted masterpiece of Oriental style architecture exists today by the wishes of 36 Brighton voters. Queen Victoria offered it to the town for £50,000, having turned down a speculative builder's offer of £100,000, but the officers of the parish were divided about whether to accept. Stormy meetings were held and the matter dragged on and on until ultimately a poll of the townspeople was taken. The result was 1,343 in favour of purchase and 1,307 against.

This magic palace full of eastern promise started life modestly enough as Brighton House, a double fronted timber framed farmhouse in the Steine. The Prince leased it in 1786 when he had debts amounting to a quarter of a million pounds. He hoped that by tactfully withdrawing from the court and the capital either the King or Parliament would settle them. But after a few months of romantic poverty with Mrs Fitzherbert he realised that he wanted a house in Brighton that would be a jewel in the Imperial diadem, a fitting palace for the great prince he knew himself to be. In the end he got it – at a cost of £1 million over the next 35 years. Henry Holland was the first architect to interpret in stone his client's dream. James Wyatt expanded on this concept and Beau Nash provided the final touches to clothe a Sussex farmhouse in the exotic dress of far Cathay.

By 1821, when the work was completed, the Prince had become King. Perhaps it was ill health, or the realisation of his dream, that stopped him coming to Brighton except for occasional brief visits after that. Now, some 170 years on, the Royal Pavilion is visited by 400,000 people every year. The Prince must surely be pleased by such appreciation of his vision.

Was it a vision or a waking dream?
John Keats

King's Apartments, Royal Pavilion

It was in the last phase of the development of the Royal Pavilion that the king's apartments were made. They are more sober, more restrained than the colourful chinoiserie of other parts of the palace for the man who would live in them was now nearly 60, overweight, suffering from gout and dropsy and oppressed by the cares of kingship. But the Chinese influence is still there – in the simulated bamboo of some of the chairs, the decorations on the black japanned writing desk, the Sevres vases on cabinets in the library which leads off from the bedroom.

Robert Jones, the designer of this suite of rooms, had chosen a design of dragons and clouds in white on a ground of bluish green for the walls. The paper used was probably hand painted although some blocks of the dragon and cloud design were made. Yellow curtains frame the recess which contains a carved mahogany bed panelled at head and foot in lilac silk and there is yellow on the doors, cornices, carvings and cushions. For the king's comfort the bed has bolsters of soft feathers, blankets of swansdown and a quilt of Marseilles lace. Also for his comfort, should she be needed at night, is a small staircase behind a concealed door leading to the apartment of Lady Conynham, the companion and friend of his later years. A similarly concealed door leads to his valet's quarters.

The king's apartments end, as the Pavilion and Brighton began, with sea bathing. A most elaborate marble and mahogany bathroom with five different baths in it was supplied with water pumped directly from the sea.

There's plenty of dippers and jokers,
And salt water rigs for your fun;
The King of them all is 'Old Smoaker',
The Queen of them 'Old Martha Gunn'.

Anon

Sunset over Palace Pier

It was not until the last year of the 19th century that Brighton's Palace Pier could be seen against the sunset. The pier building boom which started in the 1860s was virtually over when a company was formed to build a replacement to the old Chain Pier. This had acted as a landing stage for seaborne visitors, including Queen Victoria, since it was built by Captain Brown in 1822, but Channel storms had damaged it severely and it was sold to the Marine Palace and Pier Company in 1891, soon after which the last pile of its replacement was driven into place, in a high wind and with much civic ceremony, by the Mayoress of Brighton, Mrs S. H. Soper.

The Chain Pier collapsed totally on the night of December 4th 1896 – and at about the same time so did the Marine Palace and Pier Company. In 1897 an order was made for the winding up of the company and it looked as if Brighton was to be left with an unsightly half completed structure covered by hoardings at its shoreward end, until local philanthropist John (later Sir John) Howard came to the rescue. He bought the half finished structure and completed it in time for an official opening on May 20 1899. The total cost of the pier, when it was finally finished in 1901, was £137,000. It was a real pleasure pier, 1,760ft long and with a maximum width of 189ft. Its designer, R. St G. Moore, much influenced by the Oriental splendours of the Royal Pavilion, has arches of lacy ironwork everywhere topped with elaborate crestings. Later additions have been made to match. The Palace Pier theatre at the pier head, added in 1901, has a very Oriental outline, and so has the Palace of Fun in the centre which was a concert hall before 1910.

> They counted them at break of day
> And when the sun set, where were they?
> *Lord Byron*

Rottingdean

One of the few compensations for being stuck in a traffic jam on the A259 coast road between Brighton and Newhaven is the magnificent view to the south of the English Channel as the waves lap or crash against the cliffs. The road cuts most of the residents of Rottingdean off from this view although they can always savour it from the undercliff walk that extends from Saltdean to the east to Kemp Town to the west. Some 15 ft above sea level, the remains of a raised beach from a past Ice Age can be seen.

Until the advent of the motor car and coach Rottingdean was a cluster of houses and cottages around the village green, pond and church. Since then it has grown considerably but still retains its village heart. Rudyard Kipling lived here, in an 18th century house called the Elms, until 1902 when he moved to the greater privacy of Bateman's at Burwash. Another famous resident was Royal Academician Sir Edward Burne-Jones. He lived at North End House from 1880 until his death in 1898 and it was from his designs that William Morris made the stained glass windows in the chancel and tower of the village church.

When smuggling was a major Sussex industry, the villagers of Rottingdean took an enthusiastic part in it. The sails of the smock mill were used to signal to the captains of ships waiting to land contraband when it was safe to do so and more often than not it was the vicar who set the sails. The Rev Dr Thomas Hooker, who was in charge of the parish from 1792, also ran a school from his vicarage and among his pupils were Cardinal Manning and Lord Lytton. This vicarage, later altered by Sir Edwin Lutyens to become the home of another painter, Sir William Nicholson, is now a museum with rooms devoted to the work of the artists and writers who have lived in the village.

> And here the sea-fogs lap and cling
> And here, each warning each,
> The sheep-bells and the ship-bells ring
> Along the hidden beach.
> *Rudyard Kipling*

Cuckmere Haven

The watercourse which snakes through the valley between Seaford Head and the Seven Sisters is called the Meanders. Once there was a flourishing village here but it was abandoned, probably because of the Black Death, which killed off nearly half the inhabitants of the kingdom in two terrible years in the 14th century. All that is left of the village of Exceat, apart from the hill that bears its name, is a memorial stone marking the site of its church. It bears the inscription: 'Here formerly stood the parish church of *Excete* built probably in the XIth century and abandoned in the XVth century, the parish being incorporated with West Dean. The foundations were uncovered under the supervision of the Rev G W A Lawrence, Rector of West Dean and the Sussex Archaeological Society and the site preserved by the Ecclesiastical Commissioners'.

A new cut from the road bridge to the sea was made for the Cuckmere in 1846 to improve drainage and prevent flooding. At least 100 years before that the river was navigable for small barges to a mile or so above Alfriston. A gravestone in the churchyard there records the fact that John Lower (second son of Henry Lower) and parish clerk of Alfriston for 18 years, was the first person to navigate the Cuckmere River to the village. He died on 21st August 1801, at the age of 66. In 1915 the barge Iona made her last journey up river from Seaford with her usual cargo of beach and chalk. During the last war a German mine also made its way to Alfriston. On 27th October 1943 it drifted up on the incoming tide and the village was evacuated for some hours while a naval bomb disposal team defused it. The mine has been preserved near the church on the Tye.

Follow the river, and you will get to the sea.
Proverb

The Seven Sisters

The chalk cliffs which stretch from Cuckmere Haven to Birling Gap are one of the few remaining lengths of undeveloped coastline in the continually developing south east of England. They are called the Seven Sisters simply because there are seven of them, named from west to east: Haven Brow, Short Brow, Rough Brow, Brass Point, Flagstaff Point, Baily's Brow and Went Hill Brow. Beneath the sea at their base are chalk ridges and gullies supporting a rich and varied marine life – shellfish of all kinds, sea anemones, snails, sponges and limpets. And swimming around are fish with strange names like Goldsinny and Ballan Wrasse.

The Seven Sisters have been designated a Heritage Coast, an Area of Outstanding Natural Beauty and a Site of Special Scientific Interest. A Voluntary Marine Conservation Area has been set up primarily to protect the marine environment but also to encourage education, research and recreation.

In 1971 the East Sussex County Council acquired the Seven Sisters Country Park – 692 acres of the Cuckmere Valley and its adjoining coastline and set about conserving its scenic beauty and giving people opportunities to explore and enjoy it. Wisely it banned all motor vehicles except from the car parks provided. It also arranged for only sheep to graze in order to maintain the grassland in the traditional manner. At Cuckmere Haven a shallow lake was made for resident and visiting wildfowl and an 18th century barn at Exceat Farm has been converted into an exhibition and information centre. The Seven Sisters seem to be in safe hands.

Clean of officious fence or hedge
Half wild and wholly tame
The wise turf cloaks the white cliff edge
As when the Romans came.
Rudyard Kipling

The Long Man of Wilmington

Who is he – the giant man carved in outline through the turf into the chalk of the South Downs near the village of Wilmington? The 230ft high figure, said to be the largest representation of the human form in the world, has his arms outstretched and appears to be holding a staff in each hand. He was there before the Romans came – at least most historians agree that he was – although they do not agree on much else concerning the Long Man.

It has been suggested, by Alfred Watkins in *The Old Straight Track* (Abacus 1974), that he is a prehistoric surveyor, aligning points to establish a ley line for early travellers to follow. Others argue that he is the Norse sun god Baldur in the act of opening the gates to let light and warmth into the earth. Or is he one of the giants of Biblical origin? There were giants in the earth in those days 'when the sons of God came in unto the daughters of men, and they bore children to them, the same became mighty men that were of old, men of renown'. Was he perhaps a Roman soldier, a fertility symbol, a visitor from another planet or simply a figure carved on the hillside by the Benedictine monks of Wilmington Priory to indicate to pilgrims that bed and breakfast was at hand?

The Long Man is owned and maintained by the Sussex Archaeological Society.

I will go out against the sun
Where the rolled scarp retires
And the Long Man of Wilmington
Looks naked towards the shires.
Rudyard Kipling

Alfriston

This Downland village has an ancient market cross, smuggling connections, an inn covered with medieval wood carvings, a church steeped in legend and the first property to be purchased by the National Trust. With all these attractions, naturally it attracts many tourists but miraculously manages to remain unspoiled. It has always been a busy village. It was a centre of local trade from around the 15th century reaching the peak of its prosperity during the Napoleonic Wars when there were a large number of troops stationed in the neighbourhood. At about this time the Alfriston Gang were busy running contraband from Cuckmere Haven and distributing it to secret caches in the neighbourhood. Head of the gang was Stanton Collins who lived at Market Cross House, now Ye Olde Smugglers Inne, and he made good use of its six staircases, 48 doors and concealed hiding places to avoid the Revenue men when they called. But the law caught up with him in the end and in 1831 he was transported for seven years for stealing 12 baskets of barley and some sacks.

The market cross was probably first built in 1405 when Henry IV granted Alfriston the right to hold a weekly market. It has been knocked down many times since then and the present structure is not the original one but dates mostly from 1955 when its predecessor was almost totally demolished by a lorry.

The wood carvings in and on the Star Inn suggest that it was once a hospice set up by the monks of Battle Abbey for the care and comfort of pilgrims travelling between the shrines of Canterbury and Chichester.

Let nothing linger after –
No whimpering ghost remain
In wall, or bay, or rafter,
Of any love or pain.
Rudyard Kipling

Borde Hill

Merry Andrew Boord, the court jester and doctor to King Edward VI, is believed to have come from Borde Hill but no parish registers have survived from his day (1500–1549) to confirm his place of birth. He found life as a Carthusian monk too rigorous so he renounced his vows and became a doctor and writer of books on health care, travel and humour. In his *Booke of Knowledge* he states that nightingales will not sing in St Leonards Forest, which is no great distance from Borde Hill – a story repeated to this day. In 1537 a Stephen Boord of Borde Hill was brought before the Court of Star Chamber by one Richard Mathewe for attacking his wife and in 1617 Sir Stephen Boord, a major landowner in the area, was reported for causing a public nuisance by dumping logs on the road in the town of Cuckfield.

Today Borde Hill House belongs to Mr Andrew John Stephenson Clarke and its gardens are among the most beautiful in the county. It was in 1893 when he was in his early thirties, that the present owner's great grandfather, Col Stephenson Clarke, bought the property which then had a simple garden with a few good trees and shrubs. He developed it with plants raised from seeds collected by the famous plant hunters of the Edwardian era. He helped to finance some of their expeditions to the Himalayas and those of Harold Comber to the Andes and Tasmania. His greatest gift to the gardening world was the camellia Donation, raised from a cross between Camellia japonica Donckelarii and Camellia saluenensis. There are many fine examples of this camellia at Borde Hill which since 1965 has been run as a non profit making organisation registered as a charity, the objects of which are to maintain and develop its plant collection.

From yon blue heaven above us bent
The grand old gardener and his wife
Smile at the claims of long descent.
Alfred, Lord Tennyson

Carpet Gardens, Eastbourne

It was around 1904 that the Carpet Gardens first appeared on the Grand Parade near the pier at Eastbourne. Who first thought of adorning the sea front with a tapestry of flowers and fountains, grass and hedges, is not known. Before 1904 illustrations of this area show no gardens.

After 1904 they are on picture postcards. In pre-war guides to the 'Suntrap of the South', as Eastbourne was described in the 1930s, a flagstaff with a pennon advertising the adjacent Burlington Hotel was planted firmly in the middle of the gardens perhaps indicating a common ownership. The hotel's ground landlord was the 7th Duke of Devonshire, the lord of the manor and principal landowner who did so much to turn Eastbourne into a fashionable watering place. He was responsible for its tree-lined roads, its fine houses, its plethora of parks and its air of elegance which it retains to this day.

The three mile long sea front on which there is not a single shop — by order of the borough council — are two reminders of the Napoleonic Wars, the brick built Redoubt and the Wish Tower, one of the Martello towers which formed a defensive line along the south coast. The cannon on top of it has been restored and once again faces out to sea and the tower appropriately houses a Coastal Defence Museum. The Redoubt, which has given hospitality to concert parties, children's entertainers and been a roller skating rink since it was vacated by the militia, has now returned to its military beginnings and contains the Sussex Combined Services Museum.

Eastbourne has entertained many thousands of holidaymakers, among the first being three of George III's children. The composer, Claude Debussy, was here in 1905 in search of solace after the breakdown of his first marriage. Obviously he did not receive it for he wrote somewhat acidly that he found Eastbourne: 'A little seaside town, silly as these places sometimes are' and with 'too many draughts and too much music'.

To nurse the flowers, to root up the weeds, is the business of the gardener.

Bodenstedt

Forest Row

As the name indicates, this village is on the edge of a forest – the 14,000 acre Ashdown Forest – where it is quite possible to see the wood for the trees as they are interspersed with areas of heathland and rocks. In 1987 the forest was bought by East Sussex County Council for one million pounds plus from Lord de la Warr whose family had been Lords of the Manor of Ashdown since the reign of James I. The affairs of the forest are administered by a Board of Conservators from two oak-framed barns of the Ashdown Forest Centre. The third barn is an exhibition and information centre, well patronised by the hundreds of picnickers, walkers, and people on horseback who frequent the forest on fine weekends. They obviously disagree with Cobbett who in his *Rural Rides* described it as: 'A heath with here and there a few birch scrubs on it. Verily the most villainously ugly spot I ever saw in England'.

Forest Row is a main road village on the northern apex of the forest. Here the sporting peers of yesterday had their hunting lodges, to which they would return after a day in the forest in pursuit of deer, wild boar and, at one time, wolves. One of its oldest surviving buildings is the Swan for which, in 1750, a widow woman Mary Martin, paid a hen a year in rent to the Lord of the Manor for the tenancy. Holy Trinity church with its tall shingled spire was built in 1836 and opposite it is a large hall. This was a gift to the village in 1892 from Mr H R Freshfield of Kidbrooke Park in memory of his son. It still wears its original pennon weathervane incised with the letter F.

A forest is long in growing, but in a moment may be
reduced to ashes.

Lucius Seneca

The Bluebell Railway

Railways in the south were among the first to be electrified but the romance of steam still lingers on in some places. Since 1960 the Bluebell Railway Preservation Society has operated a steam locomotive service. It now runs from Sheffield Park to Kingscote (by way of Horsted Keynes) and has been a constant source of pleasure to railway aficionados or anyone who likes to live a little in the past.

Sheffield Park station was built in 1882 for the London, Brighton and South Coast Railway. It still has its oil lamps on the platform and Victorian and Edwardian advertisement panels suggesting that passengers buy Rajah cigars at 2d each and Wills Gold Flake cigarettes at 3d for 10. Horsted Keynes station is huge in size, magnificent in architecture and set in the middle of absolutely nowhere. The Southern Railway took it over in 1922 and altered it to the station pattern of those days. It is built in the style of a country house and has five platforms with glazed canopies supported by iron and timber columns.

It is, say, a fine weekend in May and one of the vintage locomotives – there really is one called Bluebell – is getting up steam at Sheffield Park's platform one for the 30 minute chuff to Kingscote. All are aboard. Flags wave, whistles are blown. Choof, choof goes the locomotive and slowly gathers speed until its voice changes into a rhythmic ch-choof, ch-choof. The line climbs 200ft from the Ouse valley through the most glorious countryside to Kingscote – and if it is the right moment in the month of May it really is bluebells, bluebells all the way.

Gathering power and purpose as he goes.
Rupert Brooke

Sinnock Square, Hastings

The Old Town of Hastings is a maze of narrow streets, twittens, walks and passages – a world away from the busy business centre and resort first popularised by Dr Baillie in the 18th century. On the seafront are the swings and roundabouts, the amusement arcades, the miniature railway, the boating pool, the candy floss and winkle stalls that attract the trippers. Away towards the Ridge are the factories and office complexes where people work with the hi-tech appliances of the present day but between Castle Hill and East Hill time has stood still. Hastings, which gave its name to the battle which was fought nearby, was once a proud Cinque Port. Now its harbour has gone and many of its old houses and churches are sunk beneath the sea. The castle on the West Hill is in ruins and St Clements Caves, that network of tunnels beneath it, are no longer used to store contraband. In the 19th century they were altered and extended by Joseph Goulding and have been a successful tourist attraction ever since.

The Old Town, however, continues to thrive, just as it did when Titus Oates was curate of All Saints in 1674 and Admiral Sir Cloudesley Shovell's old mother lived in the street leading up to that church. When he was passing Hastings on passage down Channel he asked to be put ashore to visit her. He left, it is said, with tears in his eyes. The 15th century house she lived in is still there with a preservation order on it and the name 'Shovells'.

The social life of Hastings was concentrated around the Swan Inn on the edge of the Old Town in the 18th and 19th centuries and visitors of the highest rank were lodged in the upper storeys of the houses in the High Street. The Swan was demolished after the last war and the site set out as gardens. Next to it was Old Hastings House where the poet Coventry Patmore, founder of the nearby Roman Catholic church of St Mary Star of the Sea, lived between 1876 and 1891. Its stables have been converted to a theatre.

O World! O Life! O Time!
On whose last steps I climb.
P.B. Shelley

Fishing Boats at Hastings

Until the great storm of 1287, which also washed Old Winchelsea away, the fishermen of Hastings had a harbour. Since then they have beached their boats by the tall wooden net houses in Rock a Nore. In the 1850s a total of 85 fishing boats, varying in length from under 18ft to more than 34ft, were registered in the port of Hastings. Now there are between 20 and 30 who bear the RX registration letters. The design of the net houses which are such a feature of the Stade dates back to the days of Elizabeth I. They are three storeys high and eight ft square, and the upper floors are reached by internal ladders. They were used for drying the 40 yard long mackerel nets and the 30 yard long nets used for herring fishing. Modern nylon nets almost dry themselves so the houses today are picturesque rather than practical. Nets can still be lost at sea. On February 1st 1846 one boat had such a large catch of mackerel that its nets sank and even in recent years and with modern tackle disasters can happen.

What life was like for the local fishermen in the days before diesel can be seen in the Fishermen's Museum, which is housed in a former chapel next to the net houses. On display there is a Hastings sailing lugger, *Enterprise*, built in 1909. Her heavy counter stern helps her ride the waves bow on to the beach. There are also plenty of photographs of white whiskered fishermen and even a stuffed albatross. The Shipwreck Heritage Centre nearby is devoted to disasters at sea and contains treasure salvaged from wrecks around the coast, including the *Amsterdam*. This Dutch East Indiaman came ashore at St Leonards on a January afternoon in 1748 with all guns firing. She had broken her rudder off Pevensey and the gunfire was to warn people ashore of her plight. The value of her cargo was estimated at £200,000 and, in spite of the enthusiastic efforts of looters and wreckers nearly all her 28 chests of silver were brought ashore.

I must go down to the seas again, for the
call of the running tide,
Is a wild call and a clear call that may
not be denied.

John Masefield

Bodiam Castle

Bodiam must be everyone's idea of the perfect castle – a moated, romantic fairy-tale vision in stone. It was built in 1385 by Sir Edward Dalyngrygge to guard an important crossing of the river Rother from the French raiders who had wreaked such havoc at Rye and Winchelsea. The castle, which has suites of rooms round a central courtyard for its lord, his guests, his servants and his garrison, was never actually attacked but it came close to it during the Wars of the Roses and in the Civil War when it was made undefendable by the forces of Oliver Cromwell.

The development of the cannon and the impossibility of any defence against bombardment by it made castles like Bodiam obsolete. The stronghold that Sir Edward received a licence to crenellate on October 27th 1385 was allowed to fall into decay. Its stone was pilfered to build cottages in its shadow, and even one in its courtyard, and it would have disappeared for good had not Mad Jack Fuller, squire of Brightling and noted Sussex eccentric bought it in 1829 just as it was about to be demolished.

Bodiam was lovingly restored to its full glory by Lord Curzon of Kedleston who bought it in 1916 and bequeathed it to the National Trust when he died in 1925.

> The splendour falls on castle walls
> And snowy summits old in story:
> The long light shakes across the lakes,
> And the wild cataract leaps in glory.
> *Alfred, Lord Tennyson*

The River Rother at Rye

Boats coming in from the sea can sail right into Rye on the tide and the river Tillingham and on fine weekends in the summer there are French, Dutch and other foreign flags among the Red Ensigns of these water-borne visitors. In earlier days the Strand Quay was the commercial centre of the port of Rye and cargoes would be loaded and unloaded here. As the sea has receded over the years the tidal channels of the river Rother have to be navigated for a mile or so by craft coming in from the sea at Rye Harbour. The Rother itself goes to the east of the town and through green fields occupied by sheep, cows and a line of electricity pylons to Newenden and on to Bodiam. In so doing it forms part of the boundary between Kent and Sussex.

Rye's most famous family, the Jeaks, knew the river well. The first Samuel Jeaks, born in 1623, was the author of Charters of the Cinque Ports; the second Samuel was, at 19, said to be knowledgeable about astronomy, navigation and geometry as well as Latin, French and Greek; and the third Samuel built a flying machine which nearly caused his death. Another famous Ryer, as the inhabitants are called, was John Fletcher who collaborated with Thomas Beaumont in writing *The Knight of the Burning Pestle* and other Jacobean tragedies. Queen Elizabeth I came here in 1573 and was so pleased with her reception that she said the town could be known as Rye Royal.

When the sea was calm, all boats alike
Showed mastership in floating.
William Shakespeare

Grist Mill, Rye

The sea that submerged Old Winchelsea receded from the almost island site of Rye and left it high and dry. A Cinque Port from the reign of Henry II, it is a most attractive town. Old and new buildings snuggle together on the sides of a hill topped by the parish church with its handsome 18th century clock, the quarter boys of which are now fibre glass replicas of the original figures. Everywhere there is history. The first Mermaid Inn was destroyed by the French in 1370 and they have been throwing hot pennies from the balcony of the George Hotel on Maundy Thursdays for hundreds of years. When George I was shipwrecked off Camber in 1726 he was put up by the mayor, James Lamb, in Lamb House until the weather improved. A later tenant was American novelist Henry James and he was succeeded by E F Benson, creator of *Mapp and Lucia*, those magnificent women who dominated the social life of a fictional Rye called Tilling in the 1920s and 1930s. Benson, incidentally, was also a mayor of Rye.

The town is not oppressed by its past. It still lives and works with it. The Flushing Inn with its 16th century wall paintings is now a fashionable restaurant; the grist mill on the Strand, built of sandstone blocks around 1840, is an antiques shop; and a warehouse on the quayside is a public house. Until recently the council chamber in the 18th century town hall was illuminated by candlelight and it was quite a ceremony when, as the shadows lengthened, the macebearer would solemnly lower the candelabra and light each candle in turn with a taper.

God made the country; man made the town
William Cowper